THIS PRIMARY JOURNAL BELONGS TO

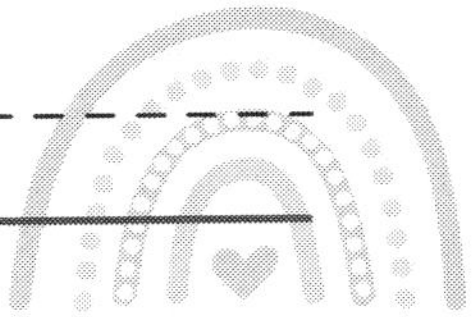

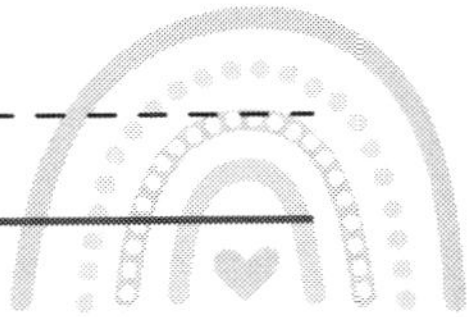

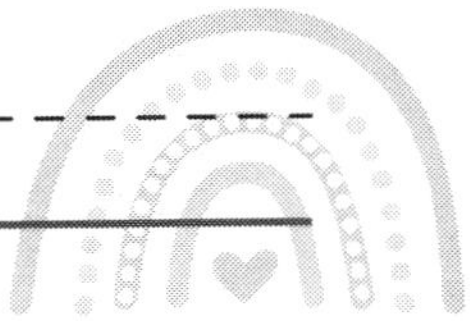

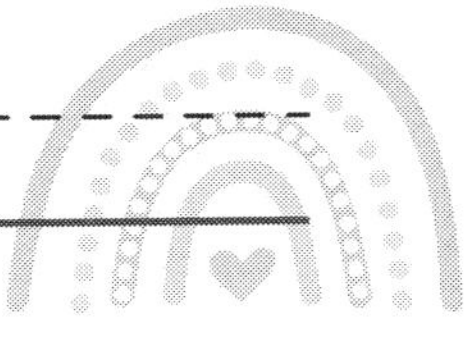

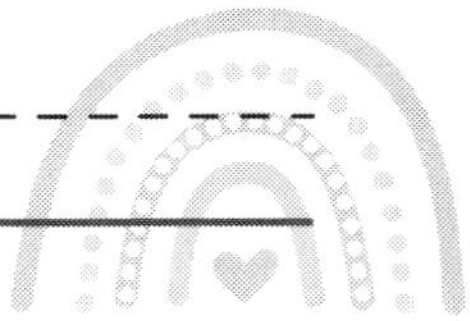

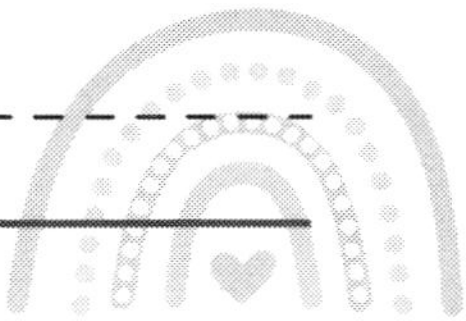

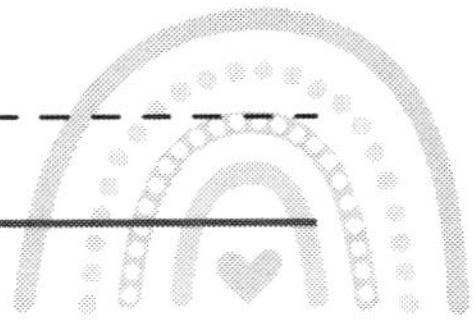

Made in the USA
Columbia, SC
03 November 2024

45575964R00061